The Dragon and the Pearl

The Dragon and the Pearl

poems by

Henry Beissel

BuschekBooks

The Dragon and the Pearl

National Library of Canada Cataloguing in Publication Data

Beissel, Henry, 1929-
     The dragon and the pearl / by Henry Beissel

Poems.
ISBN 1-894543-12-2

     1. China—Poetry. I. Title

PS8503.E39D73 2002   C811'.54   C2002-904126-0
PR9199.3.B377D73 2002

Artwork: The cover art and vignettes are based on watercolour illustrations by Arlette Francière.

Printed in Canada by Hignell Book Printing, Winnipeg, Manitoba.

BuschekBooks gratefully acknowledges the support of the Canada Council for the Arts and the Ontario Arts Council for its publishing program.

BuschekBooks
P.O. Box 74053, 5 Beechwood Avenue
Ottawa, Ontario K1M 2H9
Canada
Email: buschek.books@sympatico.ca

ONTARIO ARTS COUNCIL
CONSEIL DES ARTS DE L'ONTARIO

Conseil des Arts   Canada Council
du Canada   for the Arts

I dedicate these poems to the many people in China whose unstinting generosity and hospitality made possible a deeper encounter with Chinese culture than my six-week lecture tour to Harbin, Nanjing, Xian, Chengdu, and Beijing could otherwise have afforded me. Ultimately, it was their warmth and friendship that inspired these poems, and they are my gift to them in return.

Special thanks are due to Professor Qin Mingli, then Director of the Chinese Association of Canadian Studies, for initiating my trip; to Professor Zhu Hui for insisting that I come and teach at Sichuan University in Chengdu; and to Professor Fu Jun for inviting me to the English Department at Nanjing Normal University. I also wish to thank the Department of International Affairs of the Government of Canada for their support of my lecture tour.

I owe a special debt to Professor Lin Biguo, Director of the Centre for Canadian Studies at Sichuan University, for providing me with painstakingly accurate literal translations of the poems by Xue Tao and Du Fu which I rendered into English, and for making sure that these "free" renditions do not violate the life and integrity of the originals.

Finally, I am indebted to my wife Arlette Francière, for sharing the joys and stresses of adapting to an alien culture and for, as always, bearing with me.

CONTENTS

ANCIENT CHINESE LANDSCAPE

From narrow valleys and in faults
    and folds between slopes
mist rises and lingers across the mountain
as though the skeletal fingers of a ghost
were combing the trees. Faintly green
bushes trail their leafage down a rockface
which hides a hermit's hut
and in the secrecy of a small lake
a sacred pavilion stands
in the still water and stares
at its precise reflection
composing a mirror symmetry
the wind may ruffle
but not even a tempest can disrupt
except for its brief spell of bluster.

In the valley below
a fisherman steers his boat downriver.
Above him, from ragged drifts of mist
the mountain upheaves
scarp by spur in disjunct segments
cliffs and trees, plateaus and ridges emerging
as from a layered void
to peak at the summit above a cloudbank in a temple,
its roof birdwings folded to rest
between flights.

This is a landscape
where emptiness comes into its own.
With pale and subtle brush
China's ancient artists painted
her mountains into thought
that passes understanding.
A winding broken trail, half-hidden,
offers the mind a stone-silent path
up and down.

CHANGCHENG: THE GREAT WALL

L ike a giant petrified snake the Wall of a Thousand Li twists and turns
across plains and mountains from the Yellow Sea to the Gobi Desert.

It coils over mountain ridges, plunges down slopes and loops through
river valleys across half a continent to safeguard an empire of the sun.

No architect ever imagined so colossal a construction, sole evidence,
as far as the man in the moon can see, of homo faber on this planet.

Once upon a time it was billed as a bulwark to secure civilization
against chaos, for the barbarians are always on the other side of the wall.

Piece by piece a patchwork of ramparts rose at the whim of local potentates
and the seesaw of their enmities in the shifting sands of privilege and power.

Till Qin, the emperor who cared more for his terracotta army than for those
who created it, made the feuding lords his vassals and founded China.

He, who ordered books burnt because he would not suffer rivals and
had his own praises carved in stone tablets and erected in public squares,

imposed peace on a world of war and patronized science and the arts,
making his Middle Kingdom an empire at the centre of the universe.

Greed and ambition often are the progenitors of culture, and cruelty is seen
to be the condition for breeding an elite to eclipse the common lot.

For years and years legions of men and women were forced to labour
in all seasons to build a wall to fend off savages invading from the north.

On swift and hardy horses the Huns swept south like an ice wind from Siberia
till they were stopped by a wall five horses high, and wide as a dragon is long.

Under the punishing whip of spring storms, in stifling summer heat,
deluged by torrents of fall rain, and in the heart-stopping cold of winter,

men and women moved rocks larger than a horse, compacted earth and stone,
laid bricks and cobbles, to raise the mightiest wall the world has ever seen.

Sick and hungry, old and young, they were compelled to toil till the day's
back-breaking quota was accomplished or they collapsed from the strain.

No one knows how many workers died, how many tens of thousands
succumbed to accidents and fatigue, were killed by tribal swords and arrows.

Their bodies were pounded into the rising wall, often while still alive,
for the emperor brooked no delays and their blood helped bind the gravel mix.

This is the way a nation was united to serve a single man, Qin Shihuang,
to satisfy his appetite for power and to assuage his morbid fear of death.

A kilometer every two days for twelve long years his people raised
for him, without machines, ramparts so immense as to be invincible.

As I walked high on the cobbled terreplein, wide enough for eight soldiers
to march abreast between battlements, I heard ancient voices on the wind.

Walls, one whispered, are not worth dying for because they invite their own
destruction by inflaming those on both sides who covet what they harbor.

Walls surround wealth, added another, and wealth is not worth dying for
because it always belongs to the few who don't merit and haven't earned it.

And a third voice insisted, walls protect wealth, and the true man uses wealth
to find the path to true knowledge which is the fountain of all that's good.

The Great Wall no longer protects wealth, divides nations, or decides wars,
though Ming emperors extended it to stretch more than ten thousand li.

The Han and the Huns are tourists now, free to jointly occupy fortifications
as purposeless as its ten thousand beacon towers crumbled to heaps of rubble.

They point their cameras through embrasures to shoot misty mountainscapes
and marvel at the grandeur of this open-air museum of human pride and folly.

Then they take the cable car back down to the foot of the wall where scores of stalls
are waiting to sell them t-shirts that say: I CLIMBED THE GREAT WALL.

Souvenirs of sedan chair adventures without danger or discovery, for the glory
of the age they visit is a pile of stones and a chorus of voices inaudible to them.

INSIDE THE WALLS OF X'IAN

From atop the pagoda built to house the Buddha's
sutras you look down on the right-angled streets
of what was once the jewel of cities in all civilization,
safeguarded by the mighty walls T'ang emperors erected
to nurture, inside them, their pride and pomp with poetry
and pottery, painting and weaving, music, philosophy
and the eternal betrayals and duplicities power breeds.

But walls cannot withstand the battering-ram of time
and those T'ai-tsung and K'ao-tsung built have long
fallen, crumbled into the debris and dust of history.
Their poets are still singing, still telling the story many
a fragile scroll unravels—the story Li Po, Du Fu, Han Yu
and Li Shang-yin tell of our pilgrimage through the seasons'
pain and pleasure from darkness to what light we can endure.

Ch'ang-an was then the world's largest city and inside
its walls a galaxy of scholars, diplomats and merchants
was spinning luxury and glory about the imperial throne
while its people lived a million times over the story
of struggle and surrender, triumph and loss its artists
told with brush and pen, in stone, in bronze, in song
as it was in the beginning and will be at the end.

Ten thousand moons wore out a dynasty and diminished
the city until Ming emperors restored a smaller X'ian
to its grandeur, raising from earth bonded with lime
and glutinous rice new walls twice as high as the city's
huts and houses, once more attempting to conquer time
by giving the wheel which determines our fortunes another
turn, and in that upswing once more they flourished.

Up Nan Street through the South Gate I walked the ancient
Silk Road in the steps of camel caravans that for millennia
carried the precious cargo of wealthy merchants from and to
Arabia and every corner of Asia to barter in the market
gold-leafed gods and demons cast in bronze, bird feathers,
jade dragons, phoenixes fired in clay, silk ceremonial robes

and porcelain as exquisitely thin as a shaving of the moon—
vases, blankets, spices and sculptures, mirrors, dresses,
incense and jewelry, perfume, carpets: all the things art
and craft can fashion to delight and delude the senses
and move the mind to intimations of other dimensions.
In the shadow of the Drum Tower I walked the lanes
and alleys of the Moslem Quarter in a ceaseless rain
to listen to the heartbeat of time past and passing.

I heard across the centuries the blacksmith striking
the hot iron to hoof, smelled the heady fragrances
of wood being carved and the tawny scent of leather
at the saddle-maker's, watched the silversmith hammer
filigree and the sculptor cut marble and chase jade, tasted
the intoxicating tang of many teas, and felt the sheen
of silk stir fantasies of concubines at the finger-tips.

An hour away a magnificent army stood to attention
in terracotta, mute and aimless, underground, waiting
for orders from a dead emperor that would return them
to lives long lost forever and reassembled everywhere.
Walking in the old town I met many of those warriors,
some ready to take on the enemy, others battle-fatigued,
all of them waiting for something they couldn't name.

The rain washed X'ian that day as relentlessly
as the rain that fell on Ch'ang-an in imperial days,
but the Bell Tower now proclaims the center of a city,
not of the universe. The names, the faces have barely
changed, but the hands and hearts that lifted brute matter
for one moment beyond time and master-minded it
into ecstasies, are the same as yours, the same as mine.

If cities are the smithy where nations forge their destiny,
where imagination heats the iron of experience for creators
to place it on the anvil of their craft and hammer shape
and sense into it, then inside its walls X'ian composed
the face of China. I looked into its eyes and saw deep
inside the light dance with darkness and watched the tears
of many generations flow softly into a distant, fragile smile.

THE TERRACOTTA ARMY

You come upon them with the shock of disbelief
as though confronted by creatures born from mud,
self-engendered in clay that carried the seeds of life,
grew and molded them into human shapes to march
eastward in formation and break free from the earth,
grey figures dusty as the ground from which they emerge,
marching into speech and song, soaring towards the light,
the very dust rising up in arms against an immutable order
that confines it, mute and inert, to eternal darkness
and silence—a revolt so insolent the gods intervened,
perhaps had to intervene to uphold the cosmic law,
stopped them dead in their tracks and buried them alive.

But then the hubbub of hordes of tourists brings you to
remember that this army sprang from a child's head,
the boyish wish list of a thirteen-year-old for life-size
toy soldiers. He had the power to make his dream come true,
constraining hundreds of thousands of his loyal subjects
to labour for decades sculpting clay into warriors—
cavalry, archers, foot soldiers, officers, rank and file,
each with his proper topknot, each with his own face,
and all painted brightly head to toe, and fully equipped
with bows and arrows, lances, swords, horses and chariots—
a real army, real warriors (at least looking like the real thing)
for he did not wish to be reminded of death in his after-life.

More than two millennia have passed and the terracotta army
hasn't moved. Yet many of the soldiers have broken limbs,
others are headless, and all are hollow. So was the glory
Qin, the first Emperor, sought when he decreed the construction
of a necropolis underground, with the Yangtze and the Yellow
rivers flowing with mercury in a model of China to scale
where he could marshal his army, for he wouldn't have death
diminish his might. But the people he lorded it over rebelled
when he died, ransacked his delusions and seized his warriors'
weapons. Speechless and without orders they offered no resistance.
Shards of clay horses and men, crushed or shattered, fill the pits
where pride signed and pomposity sealed the emperor's defeat.

The six or seven thousand terracotta soldiers that survived
are far outnumbered now by tourists who fill the great hall
with chatter to hush this ancient rout. The Emperor's bones lie
mouldering in darkness a mile away in a mausoleum still buried
deep in the earth from which his artisans raised this phantom army.
If you know how to listen you can hear the voices of the past—
commands shouted, hoofs clatter, battle-cries, swords clash,
the moans of the wounded and the dying. Listen also to the softer
sounds of hands shaping clay, sculpting human features, let them
grow louder and tell you the Emperor and his army in their defeat
did win a battle, not the war, against their most implacable foe:
they may have lost their colours but they stood the test of time.

IN XUE TAO'S[1] BAMBOO PARK

We were afraid the heavy grey curtain
    would never rise on Chengdu's skies
but this afternoon the lights came up
though there were no longer enough dogs
in the city to bark at the sun. Instead, the park
burst into a thousand bouquets of bamboo
whose spindly green fingers are now sculpting
the shade into shadows tranquil and serene
where the silent voice of the ancient poet drifts
like a childhood song on the waters of the Jinjian.

Here in this bamboo-sheltered space old and young
enjoy their newfound freedom: children laughing
on their merry-go-rounds, screaming across
three generations, playing catch-me or pretend,
coloring dragons and phoenixes, while their parents
shuffle cards or mahjong tiles, or fish for carp
in the communal pond, and the old folk look proud
and share out the goodies from the picnic basket.
Furtive lovers seek the intimacy of bamboo trees
bending discretely over hidden streams and desires.

If there is sanctity here, or grace, you feel it flow
from bamboo groves whose slender resilience
cradles the sky with tenderness and fairly dispenses
the light in slim measures green and golden to all.
The sun hangs sparkling among bamboo leaves,
a festive lantern to honor this day park and people.
We move in a dance of light and shade, sharing
the community of China's people celebrating
half a century's ongoing struggle to be at home here
in this land, free and happy as in this green glory.

---

[1]Xue Tao (781-832 A.D.), also known as Hongdu, was a distinguished poet of
the T'ang period. She is said to have written over 500 poems, of which only 92
have survived.

Such is the world of which poets make their songs
until everything comes to sing, even the frustrations
Xue Tao struggled to transcend in an age more heedless
of women, their needs, their minds, their labours.
And still she can be heard singing above the green
bamboo choir, triumphant over centuries, her voice
tall as the intricate pagoda where poets used to meet
higher than the trees and talk into the dying light,
though they always knew whereof you cannot speak
you must sing, as Xue Tao sang of love and its seasons.

Later that evening, clouds fold the moon's silver fan
and the dark river runs murmuring into the night
as we drift into dreams only silence can sustain.

SPRING REFLECTIONS
(rendered after a poem by Xue Tao)

1.

Y ou're not here to share my joy when flowers bloom
    and when their petals fall you cannot share my gloom.
When does my lovesick spirit suffer most: in spring or fall?
When you're not here—that's all.

2.

I gather herbs and willow branches to tie
    into a love knot to send you with a mournful sigh.
My yearning spirit hears the birds of spring,
but they're sobbing now when they should sing.

3.

I watch the flowers age in the wind day by day
    and grieve that our reunion is still so far away.
This garland I weave is a futile exercise in art
because I cannot tie a love knot in your heart.

4.

H ow can I bear to watch blossoms unfold in a tree
    when they but bring my lover's absence home to me!
Mornings I shed tears before the mirror as I dress.
Does the spring wind know of my heart's distress?

PANDA BEAR CUB

I spotted it up in the crotch of a tree
because it seemed too large to be a fruit
and my memory bank contained no image
of any that was black-and-white and furry.

The young bear squatted on its haunches
curled against the trunk of the tree
nibbling on a fat stalk of bamboo
as though picking corn off a stretched cob.

Otherwise it sat quite still, staring down
at us with black glistening eyes set in black
ovals of fur that make them larger and
sadder, reflecting the dark forest maze.

Panda bears are too cute to convey
any sense of the beast and the wilderness
needing and testing each other to be fit
to meet nature's brutal challenges.

The human challenge is too much for any
but the tiny creatures that invade us unseen,
too much for this lumbering heavyweight
with its gentle and pacific disposition.

From inside the fenced-off parcel
of its once natural habitat, the young panda
pondered us calm as a Buddha,
watched us cluck and point and click.

I thought I caught an air of melancholy
around its plush self-containment
as though it knew its world was coming
to an end and was resigned to it.

No doubt I was projecting, for how
could a young bear know we are embarked
on the most massive extinction of species
since the last meteor struck our planet.

The panda cub climbed down from the tree
turning its back on us curious humans.
With a last long look over its stout shoulders
it dismissed us and vanished in a bamboo grove.

DU FU'S² THATCHED COTTAGE

Common people built it crudely with crude hands,
   raised it for him with its back to the city wall,
thatched it with coarse cogon grass across crooked rafters.
A hermit's hut, plain and humble, to lodge a passing poet
whom the larger world humbled on his journey every day.
He repaid his mute fellow-travellers by raising his voice
to sing their struggles and their miseries into history.

The world that disdained and dismissed the poet
in his time, sent him north and south from one exile
to another, starved him and his family, starved one
of his children to death, and left him to wander homeless
and solitary across the broken landscape of his age—
that same world ten thousand moons later rebuilt
his wretched shelter as a shrine to their own folly.

The trees in whose shade Du Fu sat have long been felled
but the river is still the same though its waters sing
to a different tune now. When the poet listened
the sun was dancing on the river, and between
crudely ploughed fields and the fresh green of rice paddies
he walked and sighed for he saw power and privilege
darken the sky and harvest only bloodshed and tears.

Since Du Fu rested and rallied here on his journey
in search of gentler shores, his people's tears have run
the river to the sea, and their blood has crimsoned
every sunset and sunrise. Have the birds listened
to his song? His hut is roomier now, a cottage
made from sturdier stuff, thatched more firmly,
more elegantly, as befits a great master of his art.

---

²Du Fu (712-770), also known as Zimei, is one of China's most distinguished
poets of the T'ang period. His extant poems number around 1500; they give a
moving account of the plight of the common people laboring under the yoke of
corrupt rulers and their brutal wars in his turbulent time.

Why is it poets must be either reviled or revered
when all they want is to be heard, not seen?
Why are their voices louder in death than in life?
Is it that we must wait for the heart of silence
to burst into song to render cruder tongues mute?
The trees know the answer; their roots fetch leaves
from a deep silence to sing and dance in the wind.

Manicured paths now wind among large groves
of trees and little streams with elegantly arched bridges,
well-tended islets of flowers and grass, playful
fountains and rocks wind and rain have carved into
age-old faces that gaze unmoved at us and this park—
a sumptuous estate fit for a palace of the rich who cast out
the poet to take his place among the poor and downtrodden.

But Du Fu's cottage and its park belong now to the people
whose sufferings he shared and ploughed into poetry.
His voice mingles with theirs, becomes one with
the leaves' choir, the water's lilt, and the melodies
of birds under bamboo and fir trees, as his body
floats forever down a distant river where he died
in a ramshackle boat that was his last and final home.

BALLAD OF THE CHARIOT
(rendered after a poem by Du Fu)

Hear the chariots rumble
    and the war horses neigh—
young and old pressed into service
    come marching this way.

They're forced to be soldiers
    armed with arrows and bow,
they must march into battle
    and fight their lord's foe.

Wagon wheels and soldiers' feet
    kick up dirt enough to screen
Xianyang Bridge which leads out of town
    and can no longer be seen.

And their parents and siblings,
    their children and wives
come rushing into the street
    fearing for their loved ones' lives.

Their feet too trample the ground
    and stir up clouds of dust
and they grieve and they plead,
    but march on the conscripts must.

Their kin clutch at their uniforms
    and try to bar their way,
they rend the skies with wailing,
    but the soldiers cannot stay.

Then one of them stops
    long enough to tell a passerby:
"There'll always be levies
    for us is not to reason why.

At fifteen I was drafted
    to serve at Yellow River fort;
at forty I'm a soldier again,
    still nothing but a warlord's sport.

I left when a mere boy,
        the village elder fixed my hair.
I came back with my hair white
        and my heart numb from wear.

Yet at my age I must fight again:
        the Emperor's wish is law to me.
For him we spill our blood in streams
        copious enough to fill a sea.

But he doesn't care a bean for us,
        doesn't care if we starve or die,
so long as we conquer land for him
        he leaves us high and dry.

What matters that our villages
        are overgrown with weeds,
so long as we can satisfy
        the Emperor's self-serving greed.

Our women may be strong enough
        to till the stony soil,
but alone they can't grow a good crop
        however much they toil.

The men from east of Mt. Hua
        are fine farmers, strong as logs—
that's why they herd us into battle
        like cattle driven by dogs.

It's good of you to ask, my friend,
        but who am I to complain?
You and I are common folk,
        we grumble and grouse in vain.

Back home our fields are wasted,
        what they yield is wretched and lean—
how are we to pay our taxes
        with a harvest so meagre and mean?

It's better to raise daughters,
        they marry and give birth;
our sons end up as soldiers
        destined to rot in the earth.

Look at the shores of Lake Kokonor
        where the bones of our ancestors bleach,
now new ghosts moan there with the old ones
        wailing in the wind on the beach."

The man falls silent and marches off
        with the others under orders to fight
for the good of the country, they tell him—
        but it's for the Emperor's pleasure and might.

NANJING SNAPSHOTS

1. Normal University, Roofs

A bevy of buildings
in the style of the ancients
squats at the centre
of this enchanted city
on green campus grounds
around a statue of Confucius
as though listening to him.

The roofs' glazed tiles
are lined with figures:
Prince Min riding a hen
at the tip of the verge.

He was hung for his cruelty
two thousand years ago.

Behind him seven fierce
and fantastic animals
fixed on one goal:
to keep him there—
a warning to other tyrants.

Chi-wen brings up the rear,
a water-loving dragon
on guard against fire.

The graceful swing
of the roofs reflects
the students' aspirations.

Higher learning
doesn't come easy
between hibiscus, bamboo,
and ideology.

The vegetation is tropical,
like the heat.
Like the ceramic
figures, students
and teacher here
in China's kiln
are fired to think.

2. Dining Out

So many invitations
to fine dining,
so many delicacies
stacked on Lazy Susans,
so many spices
to flatter the tongue—
Nanjing was a week-long banquet.

At a faculty dinner
in Harbin Arlette met
the chopstick challenge:
she picked the eyeballs
out of a steamed carp.
Applause. Eating
is a leisure activity.

In Nanjing two students,
young girls, one vivacious,
the other delicate, guides
deputized by their Department
to take us to dinner
by the Qinhuai River, facing
the Temple of Confucius.

The menu was copious:
a stream of tiny dishes,
five or six dozen dishes
each: fish, mushrooms,

duck and noodles, lamb,
green beans, pork, pickles,
bok choy, ginger and bamboo—
mouth-watering
finger food ready for chopstick-picking,
a virtual deluge of victuals,
most of them nameless
to us, some fiercely spicy,
others subtly piquant,
dulcet, savory, sour,
replete with flavors,
exotic, oriental,
never before tasted,
enhanced by zesty talk,
an orgy of the palate
shared between East
and West, an embarrassment
of riches in a country
where so many are poor.

Across the street neonlights
signal the changing times:
McDONALD's
has reached the Yangtze
River. Fast food
means fast living
brings fast bucks.
We're dining
in another age.

Eating with chopsticks
slows down the pace,
insists that you savor
what you eat
and gives a gentler
temper to dining out
than the aggressive
knife and fork.

Outside in the darkening
river in a rickety
rowboat, a man
with a landing net
on a long pole,
skims the city's
flotsam off the surface
of the water, fishes
garbage from the dancing
reflections of Nanjing's
gaudy lights and catches
along with the day's scoria
a smoldering sunset.

3. Downtown

The trees, the lake,
   the flowers and the architecture,
the river, the streets,
even its history—all
insinuate charm, charisma.

It's in the mix,
perhaps, or in the mind
and hearts of people.

They crowd
the narrow streets
lined with small shops
that wait shoulder
to shoulder for you
to call upon them.

You can get anything here:
from doorknobs to nosedrops,
a hundred different teas,
lingerie, screwdrivers,
and pirated CDs.

You can get anything
fixed too: a chair,
a watch, your shoes,
your fortune and your hair.

And always you must
barter for a price
to remove the masks
of buyer and seller
and share your humanity
with honor and esteem.

The wider avenues
are lined with plane-trees
old enough to have seen
many a conqueror come
victoriously
and go in defeat.

The strong light is filtered
by layers of leaves
to create a green ambiance
where cyclists tame
the traffic by keeping
their own sweet time.

Here time is not money
but a mode of transport
from turmoil to serenity.

Everywhere is
an endearing air:
ancient houses
with facades of wood,
ornamental gardens,
Xuanwu Lake
with its sylvan isles,
the ruins of a Ming palace,
and a Ming tomb,
the massive remnants

of an eccentric city wall—
a city kinder, gentler
than its bitter history.

The years have filtered
past miseries and cruelties
into a seasoned wine.

Government buildings
we didn't bother with.
We've seen too many
in too many of the world's
cities—functional cement
boxes as large
and as grey and grim
as the functionaries' egos
who occupy them,
and themselves in them,
with partisan duties
to the mother- and fatherland
and the happiness of all
other functionaries.

Nanjing's old world
charm has swallowed up
such dutiful edifices
to show us a human face—
though we didn't
visit the memorial site
of the rape of Nanjing:
half a million civilians
brutally slaughtered
by Japanese soldiers.

Tactfully, we were taken
to the Purple and Gold
Mountains instead.

4. The Purple and Gold Mountains

There is more than one
        narrow road
that winds up the slopes
of these mountains,
passing through bamboo
groves where green
latticework filters
the light
till there is nothing
left but the pure
glow and shimmer
of a disembodied realm.

You walk on graves.
Emperors lie buried
here in darkness,
next to the glitter
of their gold and silver
long choked in soil,
sealed into their tombs
by the heavy clamps
of a stringent earth.

You walk the spirit way,
flanked on both sides
by a cordon of camels,
elephants and tigers—larger
in stone than in life,
protectors of the dead
emperor whose ministers
and generals are gathered
life-size in effigy
to form a guard
of honor in stone
for the ugly peasant
who routed the Mongols
and declared himself
Wung-Hu:

The Heaven-Opening, Way-Implementing,
Dynasty-Founding, Pinnacle-Standing,
Greatly Worthy, Most Holy, Benevolent,
Cultivated, Righteous, Martial, Refined,
Virtuous and Successful, Exalted
Emperor—a fine tribute
to a handful of Ming
dust and bones.

We never managed
to climb the ten thousand
steps to the Mausoleum
of Sun Yatsen
who led his people
out of millennia
of slavery to warlords
and terminated
dynasties forever.

At thirty-seven degrees
in the shade you don't
climb mountains,
even up a staircase.

We missed the observatory too
where the focus is always
on the stars, on scanning
the sky, the light
and the dark, for clues
to the world we make
and don't make what it is.

5. Polished Stones

Ancient thinkers
brood in stone
statues lining
the passage to the temple
of Confucius. They think

they know what seems
to be real
is never
the real thing.

Adjacent, the display
of Nanjing's wealth
of polished stones.

Like eyes they shine
staring back at me,
daring me to try
and fathom the ages
locked inside them.

Stones chronicle
the life of minerals
far beyond the horizons
of any measurable history.

The violence of stars
roused the elements
to beget planets
and stirred them long after
what was invisible
had become hard rock,
then melted it again
in a redhot fury,
cracked and realigned
its molecular structure
in striations breaking light
into a thousand colors,
and folded a flow
of oxide and silicates
into the mix that settled
in agate, calcite and quartz
the forms and figures
that embody patterns
born in our minds.

Landscapes with rivers
and mountains, trees
and animals, surreal
in their colors, emerge
from the jumble of minerals
when you cut and polish
crystalline stones.

Grotesque shapes, fantastic
objects and fabled events—
time has concreted them
forever, hidden them
until we discover the secret
of rivers and oceans
that have tumbled pebbles
into gems for aeons.

This fabulous world may be
legendary, but its elegance
is as real as it is solid
and as solid as it seems.

Round and lucent
is the way of the spirit
that cannot be articulated
except in stone and silence.

EMEISHAN: LOFTY EYEBROW MOUNTAIN

Ten thousand steps
        twist like a slender chain of stone
thirty miles across the manifold contours of Mt. Emei
so tightly they seem hewn by nature herself
to lay out the way up
as the way down.

Under a canopy of dizzy, millennial trees
they climb the twilight
between monasteries and waterfalls
from rushing brooks to elegant pavilions
up through remote groves of fir
where the lesser panda and the silver pheasant
live furtively, and the Fairy Peak monkey
fiercely badgers the silence. In spring
exotic butterflies feast
in sudden shafts of sunlight
on an opulent diversity of spring flowers
while summer with its lush leafy cascade
darkens the interior of the forest
till the light is the color of mushrooms.

On this green and holy mountain
in the centre of China
the Bodhisattva of Pervading Goodness
has made his home,
and pilgrims in search of the way
from the base world of wanting
to the infinite peace beyond words
struggle step by step to the summit
to hoist prayer flags into the wind.

But what is the way
for the men who have no wants
because their lives are consumed
by needs?

I've watched them haul
five hundred-pound loads of stone
on their backs up the steep slopes
of Lofty Eyebrow Mountain, blood-gorged
veins bulging up their legs, clinging
to strained muscles like vines
climbing a naked tree trunk.
The pittance they earn may
content the Bodhisattva of Pervading Goodness
but not the decent people who depend on it
for the indecencies of their lives.
Nor will folk medicines of dried herbs,
berries and mushrooms, ground bones
and parched organs heaped on tables
that mark their arduous route like stations of hope
remedy their plight.

In the forest's many shades of jade
the world's contraries hang in the balance
of a peace words cannot make or break.
On their way to the summit
pilgrims rest by the pool
where the Bodhisattva's elephant bathed
and they listen to rare frogs woo
with such music in their voices
as to make the moon sing in mysterious shadows
all over the lofty forest summoning them
to other dimensions.

Past the thundering cave
at the golden summit they kneel
to await the sunrise and watch
surreal shadows dance on the clouds below
to proclaim the Buddha's glory.
Pilgrims too must come down from the mountain,
not enfeebled, like the men of burden,
but enlightened they may pass the Crouching Tiger
monastery to be reclaimed
by the flatland.

WALKING DOWNTOWN HARBIN

Time used the railway
    and the Russians who built it
to transform this lusty fishing-village
into a cement city for industry
and commerce; only the sandbank
in the middle of Songhua River
still harbors vestiges of its past
and pastoral tranquillity when
Manchuria was home to tigers.
In summer this slim island
offers a place in the sun
to those who can escape
the humid heat and traffic noise
of overcrowded tenements and alleys.
In winter you can get a taste
of Siberia whose not too distant
chill reaches from the other side
of the Black Dragon River to raise
goose-bumps on the city's skyline.
Irreligious onion domes
and patriotic ice sculptures record
Harbin's brief brush with beauty
that has fled its teeming streets.

If there are laws here
to regulate transport and traffic
they cannot be put into words.
No stop signs impede the flow
and the scattering of traffic lights,
when and where they work,
are ignored or they cause bulges
jammed with vehicles and people
that quickly gorge the streets
on both sides and in both directions
before bursting and roaring at each other
like two opposing avalanches

sweeping cars buses and bicycles
trucks and trailers taxicabs
and tractors oxcarts pedestrians
handcarts and chauffeured limousines
in a sudden inextricable surge
in every direction roadways permit.
They merge, mingle and diverge again
with everything and everyone, miraculously,
still on the move, still intact, still alive,
and still more miraculously, everyone
patient and philosophical as Confucius.

Only I, the stranger, am torn
between ochlophobia and road-rage.
I feel pushed and pulled
trapped in a slide of people
moving to unknown ends
though no one touches me
and there are only smiles
as every head turns to stare
at this white-haired pink-faced figure
tall and alien as an extraterrestrial
while I wait for the slam and crash
of pile-up collisions as vehicles lurch
forward whose drivers have eyes
backward and sideways only for me.
But horns honking and bells ringing
they continue on their imperturbable way
to melt anonymously into memory.

Their way is my way too
and I must accept that in a city
of multitudes and technology
where crossing the street
is a matter of life and death
walking is a malapropism.

MANCHURIAN TIGER

Soundless the tiger's
footfall that hushes
fauna and flora with the force
that strikes blood
to elevate life.

Majestic cat,
distant and disdainful,
bringing the mystery
of remote wildernesses
to mind.

Never was there beast
more limber, more sinuous,
more alert, stalking
prey in the underbrush
of twilight.

Under the silken fur
muscles move in waves
supple as the wind,
ripple more softly
than a brook.

An integrity of muscles
honed by millennia of hunting
with a pounce to fell an ox
yet light as a breath
drifting through grass.

Paws padded
to silence forest floors,
a tiger makes even dry twigs
and crisp leaves pliant
to his stealth.

His body glides
through evenings like reeds
bending to a breeze,
blending short fur
with tall grass.

I look in his eyes
and see deep in the dark
the glow of ancient green
jungle fires about to leap
into flames.

Something is roused
below memory's horizons—
some image aeons etched
into scars of gashed flesh
and traumas of flight.

If only I could read
the map time has
drawn across his face,
pick up the clues
on his retina.

Tiger eyes stare
at me burning with
a rapture that chills my blood
for it feeds on fears
older than reptiles.

What is it you hide
behind those languid eyelids,
behind the bars on your fur,
inside your striking silence—
what terrible secret?

For never was beauty
so hauntingly matched,
so brutally wedded
to terror as in the tiger's
swift fur and claw.

The weight of brute
power in the scales of
grace measures the mystery
in nature's savage
triumphs.

Solitary tiger—
natural-born ruler
who wields the power
of life and death
according to the law.

Even here
in his Manchurian captivity
a tiger will not surrender
dignity to the dictates
of habitat.

A chain fence
confines his prowl
to the forest in his eyes
but he stalks the wild
domain inside

his spirit untamed
passes into oblivion,
leaving us, the alien sky
and the grassland
to the wind.

ZIJINCHENG: THE FORBIDDEN CITY

The forbidden city is forbidden no more.
Time has stormed across its moats, breeched
walls ten meters high and buried the soldiers
with the swords and lances that defended it.

Imperial halls and palaces are trodden now
by those whose ancestors' sweat and blood
built them for self-made lords and masters to enjoy.
The egalitarian clock struck down all privilege.

I entered along the meridian (the ruler's seat
in an empire of the sun is always in its zenith),
walked through the gate opening to the south
(through which emperors passed twice a year

into high noon) and stepped into the stale splendor
of a petrified past, a museum of bygone glories and
their shame. Where once nobles trembled lest
they offended I photographed schoolchildren laughing.

They'd come to see their history without reverence,
to know the stories of their mothers and fathers
whose every twist and turn recorded someone's fall
or fortune by the same rules by which they played.

It's no child's play to build a city though
we destroy them like so many children's toys.
Who knows how many cities rose and fell here
before and after the Kingdom of the Yan

until ten thousand moons after its demise
the Mongols razed Zhongdu, capital of the Jin,
and Khublai Khan built Dadu in its blood-
soaked place as a centre of the arts and learning.

Thus empires, like their rulers, come and go
by the stroke of a sword or a pen, by fire,
folly, or by random chance their fate is sealed—
yet blind ambition rebuilds them for eternity.

A million men and women labored for a decade
to build Beijing, city of the north, laying foundations,
erecting walls, constructing gateways and roads,
all on right angle grids by the ruler and the whip.

And here, in the middle of that supreme city
of the Middle Kingdom they built this other city,
sanctum sanctorum of emperors and their entourage
of concubines and eunuchs, soldiers and sycophants.

As I drifted in a cold October wind from gate
to gate among great halls, palaces and pavilions,
in a throng of tourists descended from those who
were forbidden to enjoy the grandeur they created,

a great silence suddenly reached across centuries
and swept the huge squares clean of people
and of sounds, and in that void of stone and wind
it was as though my eyes detected voices—

voices of command and flattery, conspiracy,
entreaty, denial and submission, ricocheted
off stone-carved balustrades, bronze lions
incense burners, clouds chiselled into marble,

and gathered in ten thousand sumptuous rooms
to scatter and die among imperial knickknacks
and magnificently attired ghosts no one could forbid
to remain after they lost their games with their voices.

I stood on a stone bridge in the Great Within
and stared into the still Golden Water Stream
bending like a Tartar bow before the gate
that leads to the Hall of Supreme Harmony.

And I smelled the sweet-burning incense,
heard the bells of gold and jade toll
as the emperor mounted the Dragon Throne
to celebrate the New Year or his birthday.

Flanked by two cranes in cloisonné enamel
he sits in the thatched hall under hipped double roofs
between gilded ornamental walls and pillars
resplendent in robes woven of silk, silver and gold

while outside on the terrace a sundial measures
the hours whose passage not the sculptured tortoises
nor all the wealth of emperors, nor the sword's brute
power that procured it, can delay by even one minute.

A cold gust crumpled the images on the surface
of the water and blew them under the bridge.
Pity the suffering of those who pay the price
of magnificence: time's mills grind all to dust.

But the emperor would have none of that.
He sat midway between the North Star and
the sun at the centre of all things where
the immortal dragon conferred divinity on him.

He was the pivot on which the cosmos turned.
Guarded by the lion and assured by tortoise, crane
and phoenix of his longevity, he lived in mythic
dimensions playing with the dragon's sacred pearl.

Only two seasons brought him out from legend:
summer, when he moved his court to the palace
and gardens on the shores of Kunming Lake,
and spring, the first month of the lunar year

when he emerged like a golden peacock, carried
in a glorious sedan to the Temple of Heaven to pray
under a most exquisitely timbered painted ceiling,
under a blue-tiled round roof, for a plentiful harvest.

But prayer cannot heal injury or right injustice.
Behind the many walls of his private city
the emperor fell into a stupor of splendid isolation
and left the empire to be corrupted by his eunuchs

until the people found their own heroes to cut loose
from oppression and fight for their lives and liberty.
Cities went up in smoke and the last empire choked
to death in its own blood. Sic transit gloria mundi.

I passed through the Gate of Terrestrial Tranquillity
to enter what were once the Imperial Gardens.
The harmony that eluded emperors was palpable here
where man and nature joined forces to transcend

a world that makes us strangers in the larger world.
I walked winding paths among flower beds,
bushes and trees that wove the four seasons into one
rain-harvesting and wind-gathering landscape.

Stone sculptures assembled from rocks hauled down
from mountains and up from the bottom of lakes
spoke to cypress trees bending over them
as earth and sky met to exchange perpetual vows.

I sat by the fountain and saw in the water play
the rise and fall of cities and empires.
Beyond the trees the imperial yellow shone
on glazed roofs like so many setting suns.

The walls around the forbidden city were painted
a divine vermilion, though the worlds they girdled
were not made in heaven. Rich in love and pain, as any
tragicomedy, they perished for better and for worse.

I left by the gate where Mao's picture hangs suggestive
of emperors, and felt relieved from the burden of history
to find myself under an open sky whose light promised
a path to true cities of the mind forbidden to no one.

THE DRAGON AND THE PEARL

One evening I stood on the banks of the Yangtze
and listened to the river whispering to the sky
that the dragon is master of all the world's water
and that water is the secret of his immortality.

And the river spoke of the rain that fed it,
of the oceans that it must feed in turn, and
of the wheel the dragon keeps turning that loops
life from the sea through the clouds to the land.

I know that this water wheel flies in the face
of inertia, powered by the sun to spin life
into trillions of compound forms and variations
as the elements permit and chance may inspire.

The same rain that quickens nature's pulse
fills every farmer's barn and stable
and bathes every heart in everlasting hope,
thus determining our fortunes and our fate.

So China's dragon is an envoy of the gods
bringing to earth the magic of water
that transforms all that it touches: stone
into fruit, fruit into flesh, and flesh into mind.

Snake and eagle, tiger and carp—
all creatures peak in the dragon's mind
and he distills from them supreme virtues
that grow inside his head into pearls.

Opalescent pearls—dragons spit them out
and they plop into the world as into a lake
running concentric circles outward to pattern
the nation's fabric in an image of harmony.

Such were the gods' gifts to emperors,
and they took them in their pride, forgetting
the yin over the yang of power and wealth,
for the dragon had cast the pearls before swine.

Some say these pearls were forged in the flames
that burnt Buddha's body back to ashes in nirvana.
You can still see the fire in the pearls' iridescence
where it blends with water in the spray of waves.

Emperors and their empires have vanished into history,
but majestically the waters of the Yangtze flow on
winding down from the highlands of Tibet to rush
through gorges across Sichuan into the Yellow Sea.

I watched the river that no longer harbors dragons
nor nurtures pearls, gently rock the sun to sleep,
carrying the stories of our madness, regardless of rank,
triumph or defeat, forever and far out to sea.

TIANANMEN: SQUARE OF HEAVENLY PEACE

This vast open space was once the last station on the path of mortals
to the forbidding emperor sitting in his forbidden palace on the Dragon
Throne behind walls within painted walls within squares of walls
at the centre of the universe to mediate between heaven and earth.

On the checkerboard of power this was the least important square—
a large field cleared to dust, perhaps to drill and array the Ming army
or to summon peasants and artisans, craftsmen and traders, to cater
to the emperor's every pleasure at table, in state, at prayer and in bed.

Perhaps petitioners waited here in wind and rain, sunshine and snow,
with gifts to humbly plead their case in the court of bribes and favours,
present them to the lowest in the order of the anointed who could pass
through the Gate of Heavenly Peace into the city forbidden to others.

There were fairs here, surely, country fairs to mark the feast of emperors
and gods: that potpourri of jugglers and acrobats, sword-swallowers
snake-charmers, fortune-tellers, tent shows, garish music and carrousels
that makes young and old know the world over that life is good.

Were there summary decapitations here too, enforcing fealty and deterring
revolt? Whatever blood was spilt has long been buried with the people's sweat
under acres of cement squares that have been hosed down, washed clean
by government decree, and yet ring hollow not only to goose-stepping soldiers.

Outside the palaces of the powerful order and freedom always clash
for both make legitimate claims. But the chains of tanks don't bind a people
together, any more than camps do, or than slogans will clothe or feed the poor.
The yin and yang of government are the hearts and minds of the governed.

Under the thousands of imperial and revolutionary moons this square has grown
larger, for despots suffer from elephantiasis of self-esteem that distorts
grotesquely their true worth for it inflates the puffed face of all power.
And they build plazas, avenues and mansions fit for the giants they are not.

I walk across the bustle in Tiananmen Square looking for Heavenly Peace
and find only the voices of tourist guides touting achievement by statistics,
confusing what is big with what is great. The echo in this cement landscape
is empty of the promises courage holds before it is poured in concrete.

Winter winds blow fine sand from the Gobi desert into this blustering space.
Between Mao's proclamation of the new republic and his mausoleum
my steps crunch a gritty grandiloquence. I watch the sun set blood-red
over the Great Hall of the People that is still waiting for its proper assembly.

PEOPLE, PEOPLE EVERYWHERE

Multiply the population of every village, town and city in Canada by a factor of fifty and you'll begin to feel the crush of people, people everywhere. You expect to visit a village in China that harbors a Taoist temple or some ancient statue of Buddha, and you find yourself instead in the traffic chaos of a city inhabited by millions, a city you've never heard of, and there are more of these than your atlas shows or your geography teacher dreamt of.

People, people everywhere. In the old core of the city they're packed into picturesque and ramshackle cottages infested with the woes of want, where generations share spaces that make a mockery of privacy and discretion, and where facilities refers to the survival skills of the occupants. Or they're stacked ten storeys high in apartment barracks lined up like beehives (and with as much traffic and room) or clustered to form communities of anonymous multitudes.

People, people everywhere crowding the main streets of China's cities like colonies of ants on the move, emerging from some inexhaustible underground well of creation, or as though they sprang to life from every handful of dust on the sidewalks, swept up by irresistible currents into streams and counterstreams of bodies, eddying at intersections in a melee before spinning off on predetermined routes to flow without haste or hurry toward an ill-conceived destiny.

People everywhere moving in all directions, people on foot and people on and in all manner of vehicles: bi-, tri- , and motorcycles, horse-, mule- and oxcarts, cars of every make, model and vintage, home-made crates on wheels powered by toy engines spewing black smoke and white steam as though they were about to erupt. You don't dare gesture too broadly or too suddenly change direction and step out of the peristaltic flow for fear of collision or mutilation.

Is this the flow Confucius urged upon people everywhere?
In China people flow through the din and fumes of traffic
as calm and unruffled as a troop of saffron-garbed monks.
Did I fail to see the soft order beneath the harsh reality?
Smiling and spitting, they pay tribute to the yin and yang
of contradictory worlds, holding in their hearts the balance
between a reckoning with the past and the price of the future,
between the high-rise city and the humble holy mountain.

THE GRAND BUDDHA OF LESHAN

Carved out of rufous cliffs
the Grand Buddha sits inscrutable,
his head high as birdflight,
and contemplates what passes.

Nothing surprises him
for his mind is a rock
and nothing is palpable
to him who contemplates it.

Before his moveless eyes two rivers
enter each other and become one,
their waters rushing and roiling
in their flight past the city to the sea.

His ears tall as trees,
and as open, the Buddha listens
and hears the distress and anguish
desire brings on all things.

If his heart too were not
chiselled from stone
surely it would break
in a burst of compassion.

He has watched ten thousand
moons wax and wane
and the world's pain
has remained the same.

His smile has slimmed down
for he is no god, and cannot
conceive of a god turning
a wheel of suffering to eternity.

But the eightfold path is steep,
steeper than the vertical steps hewn
into the sides of the cliff down
to the feet of the silent Buddha

who gazes beyond the river
at a paradise where all coveting
vanishes into something less
than air or light or meditation.

Across the river dusk creeps
into the cobbled streets of the old town
where people sit at sidewalk tables
to share a hotpot meal.

Neither the turbulent waters
nor the tranquil Buddha
trouble their shared dream
that what they perceive is real.

They savour the food and talk
of what came to pass today
and what tomorrow is to come
as darkness gathers them in.

The Grand Buddha withdraws
into the night and comes to rest
in the puzzle of his being
there or anywhere at all.

He leans against the iron-shot cliffs
and never closes his eyes.
He has seen too many worlds pass;
nothing can make him blink.

Where the Min and Dadu join forces
to turn the heavy wheel of the world
the Grand Buddha's mind towers
above them, ten thousand stories tall.

The rivers have come to the Buddha
knowing he has nothing to say to them,
nothing to cast upon their torrent waters
except a single lotus flower and his thin smile.